Pilgrimage to Renewal

Jo win

These stories
are true as
are yours

Herb Brokering

Pilgrimage to Renewal

For Individuals, Small Groups, and Families

by Herbert F. Brokering

Winston Press

Cover design: Maria Mazzara-Schade

Photo credits: Jean-Claude Lejeune—p. 6, *Minneapolis Tribune*—p. 10, Vernon Sigl—p. 20, Randy Dieter—p. 36, Jean-Claude Lejeune—p. 50, John Arms—p. 62, Vernon Sigl—p. 76, Vernon Sigl—p. 86

Library of Congress Catalog Card Number: 79-65029
ISBN: 0-03-053791-6

Printed in the United States of America

5   4   3   2   1

Winston Press, Inc.
430 Oak Grove
Minneapolis, Minnesota 55403

Contents

Preface

Pilgrimage to Renewal is about you, about us. It tells about people on journeys, and we are all on journeys—many journeys. We are forever traveling to places outside us and inside us, to times past and present and future. We are forever exploring our own and other people's deepest feelings and insights.

This book invites us to be not just travelers but pilgrims. Travelers become pilgrims when they make a holy journey, a journey transformed by faith. When we look with the eyes of faith, all the ground we walk on becomes holy ground; all the people and all the common sights and sounds and happenings become miracles.

Pilgrimage to Renewal invites us to join the huge pilgrim throng that has been journeying down the ages—from Abraham setting out for an unknown land, to Jesus showing us the path of redemption, to our brothers and sisters searching for a richer, happier life.

Among the pilgrim band, Jesus is the traveler who is himself the very Way we journey from death to life. "Come, follow me," he invites us; "he who follows me will not walk in darkness, but will have the light of life."

It is no accident that *Pilgrimage to Renewal* uses many of the methods that Jesus used to awaken us and to plumb our inner depths:

mysterious, simple-sounding stories that open up huge vistas; images of water and bread and flowers and birds that put us in touch with our most profound longings; parables that challenge our easy way of life; rhythmic language that makes us want to dream, sing, or march happily along with our fellow pilgrims.

You can use this book in many ways. Use it for your individual pilgrimage—for solitary reflection, meditation, prayer. Use it with your family at home—for reading, discussion, family prayer. Use it with study groups or prayer groups. Use it in Advent to prepare for the Savior's new and fuller coming. Use it for your Lenten journey to the cross and to Easter—that passing over from death to life which is the heart of the Christian way.

Lord of people on the way

Lord of people on the way,
Listen as we humbly pray:
Be the road we walk today,
You who called yourself The Way.

When we wander here and there,
On the verge of deep despair,
Drive away the clouds of care,
Make our days both warm and fair.

Lord, you made the flood go down,
Set the ark upon dry ground,
Made the wretched leper sound,
Sought the sheep till it was found.

Make your pilgrims wise and brave,
You whose strong arm bent to save
Peter from the wind and wave,
You who conquered death and grave.

Lord of people on the way,
Listen as we humbly pray:
Be the road we walk today,
You who called yourself The Way.

Chapter 1

Pilgrimage beginnings

A Lenten journey

It was Lent—pilgrimage time. The
congregation could not pay for a journey to
Jerusalem. So they met and talked about
pilgrimages they could afford.

They decided to do simple things together
each week. As they did them, they journeyed
to places within themselves.

So on Ash Wednesday they took ashes and
began their journey to Jerusalem and to
Easter. With sweet oil they marked the heads
of the young and promised them affection.
They touched each person with water and
the sign of the cross. It took an hour. And it
was quiet. They had time for a pilgrimage of
the mind and the spirit. They remembered
weddings, funerals, and baptisms. They
recalled holidays spent alone and with others.
They thought about places where they'd
traveled, sung, argued, and voted. And they
sighed as they remembered days and weeks
of waiting and wishing. Each person
contemplated something real inside the world
of self.

Another time they heard the words of
Mark 14:51-52.

A certain young man, dressed only in a
linen cloth, was following Jesus. They tried
to arrest him, but he ran away naked,
leaving the cloth behind.

Then they made pilgrimage cloths and put
the mark of the cross upon them. The cloths

12

reminded each person of the young follower of Jesus. They talked about being brave and about fleeing. As they put these cloth garments on each other, they made warm comments. And they thought.

Later, they sprinkled seed outside, for soon it would fall through the melting snow and turn the earth green. They talked about new life and growing.

One week they read and told stories about waiting and about hope. They recalled how long the Jews had waited for the Messiah. And they prayed.

Once they hung bunches of grapes overhead. As they reached high for them, they said prayers of thanks. It was Maundy Thursday. Then they went to a table to eat and drink homemade bread and wine. And they sang.

Throughout their journey, these people had stored some souvenirs of their Lenten pilgrimage in the many compartments of a memorabilia box. During Holy Week they recessed this box into the center of a wooden cross and placed it in the chancel. On Good Friday they nailed a large board over the memorabilia box. They thought about suffering and death.

On Easter morning they drilled round holes into the board, one for each section of the box. The cross with its box of pilgrimage souvenirs became a birdhouse. They put it in the churchyard. The birds come and go on their own pilgrimages, and the cross is their home. The pilgrims had given of themselves. Their souvenir box had received a new life.

It was a long Lenten pilgrimage, and much of the journey took place inside their spirits, but it nourished body, mind, and soul.

How does a pilgrimage get started?

The desire for a pilgrimage comes from the inside. Inside you is the child who asked "What's dat?" a thousand times. Inside you lives the one who probed, poked, jumped rope, somersaulted, waved to birds in flight, and clapped hands in delight. The child in you keeps you moving with your imagination and lets you see with the eye of emotion. The insights and surprises and double takes come from within. The drive needed for pilgrimage stems from the curiosity of the mind.

A pilgrimage depends on a questing heart. It keeps your feet on the move. The spirit keeps the momentum of the journey going. The head and the heart together make the pilgrimage more than a hike.

Recall images from your childhood. Talk about places you went when you were young. Who went with you on these youthful journeys? What did you do? What did you say? Let the child in you get you started again.

Wandering people

The story of God's wandering people began with Abraham. The Christian's pilgrimage has its roots there too.

Abraham's pilgrimage meant more than moving from place to place. Each call from God gave Abraham another opportunity to see himself more clearly. On each new journey this pilgrim learned something new about his faith. You can read about his pilgrimage in the New Testament letter to the Hebrews.

A Christian's pilgrimage also includes this internal pathway. Once I asked someone, "Where are you going?" The answer came quickly, "I don't even know where I came from." The interior journey can become a Christian's search for identity. Pilgrims often ask, "Where are we?" Some also inquire, "Who am I?"

How pilgrims travel

There are famous and popular pilgrim places to go. To the Holy Land or to Canterbury. To Rome or to the home of Saint Francis at Assisi in northern Italy. Such pilgrimages can be memorable experiences.

But since not everyone can make the real trip, many pilgrims imagine and pretend and dramatize their pilgrimages. To think about traveling to different places can also be a pilgrimage, whether to Jerusalem or Lourdes, to a jail, a factory, a war memorial, a cemetery, a monastery, or a Christmas party.

Pilgrims are alert on their journeys. When they walk about a new city—real, imagined, or remembered—they see more than what the guide points out. They notice things on their own. Perhaps they see something they've read about. Or maybe they hear a child cry and know human need is also there.

Pilgrims look twice. They see beneath the surface. They see the rainbow and think of promises and happy endings. They feel the wind and think of the Spirit that gives life. They notice a deep joy in wrinkled faces. They feel loneliness and recall Jesus' words: "I come when you are with the lonely."

Pilgrims see the ordinary as extraordinary. A face, a bird in flight fighting a strong wind, a sunset coloring the clouds belching from a factory smokestack, a grandfather's old boots, a hillside where Jesus preached—in all of these a pilgrim sees something remarkable. Pilgrims expect special sights, and that is why they find them.

Crusaders

In the Middle Ages, before Columbus came to America and before Copernicus said the earth was round, there were crusades.

For some a crusade was a religious war. These crusaders enlisted out of a deep commitment of faith and made great sacrifice. For others a crusade was an adventure, a long party, or a chance to loot. But the original idea was to free the cities of Jerusalem and Bethlehem and the grave of Jesus from the rule of non-Christians.

The cross was the official badge of the crusader pilgrims because their journey was for Christ and perhaps even unto death. Rescuing the Lord's sepulcher or birthplace was, after all, dangerous business. And so they wore the cross on their capes; they inscribed it on their weapons; they decorated their shields and their banners with it.

Crusades were often launched by the preaching of a pope or holy person at a rally. But the exhortation made it more than a pep rally. The Gospel gave the pilgrims energy to begin their journey.

Pilgrims need courage to get started. Who gives the rally speech today? Who stirs up the spirit? Who touches the imagination? Who sends the pilgrims on the way?

Could a child launch such a pilgrimage? Could someone you know stir up such devotion? Could it happen over the radio? Can you imagine such a pep talk given by a prisoner? Would it excite you more if the speaker were someone on death row?

Could a nun or a monk influence people through silent prayer? Could a letter from a needy stranger get people to move in order to achieve a goal?

What story from the Scriptures might get a pilgrimage on the way? What did Jesus say or do that might have such power?

What could *you* say if you wanted to move people to become pilgrims on a journey?

What, dear Christ, have we in store?

All go through a single door,
barefoot feet and little more,
sun that shines and clouds that soar.
What, dear Christ, have we in store?
Grace and peace and more and more.

All go through a single door,
joining two and three and four,
pilgrim feet on street and floor.
What, dear Christ, have we in store?
Bread and wine and more and more.

All go through a single door,
queens and kings, and rich and poor,
going off to dance and war.
What, dear Christ, have we in store?
Hope and life and more and more.

All go through a single door;
wind will blow and waters roar,
spirit whirl and spirit soar.
What, dear Christ, have we in store?
Fire and light and more and more.

The paschal lamb

The paschal lamb was part of Israel's yearly
pilgrimage to Jerusalem. It was their offering.
Sometimes the lamb was a family pet that
made the journey with them, to be offered in
their place. Often they loved it; it was like a
member of their family. So when it died,
they felt they died too.

But the lamb was more than an offering. It
was like a mirror in which the people could
see themselves. In and through the lamb they
saw themselves saved.

Getting involved in a sacrificial journey can
teach me who I am. Jesus, who is both the
suffering and the victorious paschal lamb, can
give me that inner self-awareness.

O little lamb of Bethlehem,
caught in the bush of Abraham,
praise be to thee, dear paschal lamb.
O tell me who I am, I am.

O little lamb of Bethlehem,
give me a crown, a diadem.
Praise be to thee, victorious lamb.
O tell me who I am, I am.

Chapter 2

Pilgrimage sights and sounds

Begin with singing

Pilgrims sing along the way. Once we went on a singing pilgrimage for a whole year. Still, we did only a little of what we had planned.

We sang ten hymns, each one with a different instrument. Imagine singing "Beautiful Savior" with a saxophone and "O Sacred Head Now Wounded" with a flute.

In ten houses we heard the family's favorite music. Some of the music was shared around a piano; some came from stereo records. Some songs were in languages we didn't understand.

Then we practiced with other choirs, and we sang in each other's churches. One holiday we made a choir pilgrimage through the city streets.

What are your favorite pilgrimage songs? Have you ever sung Christmas songs at Easter time and Good Friday hymns along with Christmas songs? At one festival the people sang songs for each part of the church year.

Who wrote the words and composed the music for these hymns? Can you imagine their journeys of faith by reading and singing their songs? Are their journeys all alike?

Are the words in hymns and religious songs sometimes difficult to understand?

Have you tried to see pictures inside the words, to imagine where the writers were and what they felt? Perhaps your imagination will take you to other countries or to inner places—to new feelings and new insights.

Signs

In the water and the bird,
in the reading of the word,
in the breaking of the bread,
in the waking of the dead,
in the begging at the door,
in the clothing of the poor,
in the bursting of the wall,
in the healing of the fall,
in the making of the light,
in the angels of the night,
in the crying in the stall,
in the living of us all,
in the shaping of our love,
in the coming of the dove,
in the washing of the feet,
in the suppers that we eat,
in the parting of the sea,
in the life that comes to me—
Lord,
we see the signs of thee.

Water

Water flows along our way;
it quenches thirst and cools the day,
washes tears when children weep,
soothes the feet and makes them leap.

Water comes as falling dew,
wakes the flower, wets the shoe.
Hydrants open in the street;
children splash and bare their feet.

Water stands along the walk,
mixed with fingerpaint and chalk.
City water, country spring—
hear the pilgrims laugh and sing.

Refreshed

It was summer, and it was warm. Many
people were moving along a pilgrimage route.
They were sweaty and thirsty. But there was
nothing to drink, and there were no fans.
The air was still.
   Then winter broke into the summer heat.
On the mountainside they came upon a patch
of snow. Dozens of snowballs moved from
hand to hand. They didn't throw them away
or crush them to pieces in a brief moment of
fun. They savored them, for they cooled

their hands and their whole bodies. The pilgrims were refreshed.

They kept going, and pictures of winter times flashed before their eyes. On this summer pilgrimage the seasons had met in the sweaty palms of hands and in the far reaches of memory. One season had ministered to another in the lives of pilgrims on the way.

Story beats

Find the heartbeat of someone's pulse. Beat it out by tapping your foot. Drum the clear rhythm for a group. Add the sound of their snapping fingers or tapping toes. Keep the rhythm as regular as the heartbeat. Add the sound of wood. Thump your fingers on church pews. Or on a stump or log nearby. The sound is dense and strong. Keep the rhythm steady.

Sustain the sound, and tell the story of Abraham's journey with Isaac up Mount Moriah. The beat is Abraham's walking. Imagine the father's feelings, or the son's.

When he lifts his knife to slay his son, double the beat. It is Abraham's heartbeat. Feel how fast it pulses. How it transforms the pilgrimage.

When God says to Abraham, "No, don't slay your son," cut the beat in half. Quiet Abraham's heart.

When Abraham descends the mountain with Isaac to tell Sarah the good news, double the beat again. They are running. The beat is the footfalls of a grateful man and of a thankful son.

Try this kind of rhythmic accompaniment with other journey stories. Try it with Moses. Try it with Jonah. Rhythmic involvement in the pilgrimage of biblical characters adds freshness and excitement to the stories. And it unites you with the group.

Shhh

Clowns are moving about, whispering to other clowns who only listen. They put their fingers to their lips as a sign of *Sh.*

A crashed auto sits halfway across the sidewalk. An ambulance with its lights flashing is there. The attendants stand by attentively and are still.

With her arm around a sleeping child, a mother sits on the doorstep on a summer day.

A large gift-wrapped box sits between two candles.

Clowns hoist signs that ask *Will it happen?*

Over a table set for one, but without food, hangs a placard with the words *Will Jesus come?*

The empty rocking chair, with a shawl draped over one of its arms, moves gently back and forth on the flatbed of a truck.

Clowns get the pilgrims to hold hands.

Soft harmonica and flute sounds fill the air along the route. A woman hums "Jesus Walked This Lonesome Valley" while a man does a softshoe. A minister kneels in prayer beside a cross.

A deaf-mute choir signs a prayer hymn. A paraplegic uses retrained toes and feet to paint on canvas.

Clowns mark the ears and eyes and mouths of the pilgrims with the sign of the cross and with oil.

Large balloons everywhere carry the word *Sh.* A group sings "Sounds of Silence."

Someone ties a cluster of balloons to a cross. Some say *Sh.* But a new word emerges—*Shalom.*

Pilgrim farmers

Farmers are pilgrims too. They walk their fields in spring and in fall—forever between harvest and seedtime, seedtime and harvest.

Homesteading and passing on a farm from generation to generation is also a pilgrimage.

What does one do when a farmer quits, or dies with no one to take up the reins? What happens at the end of a farming pilgrimage?

There's usually a farm sale. It can be a celebration—a time of remembering and rejoicing. There's always coffee and food and conversation. The loud and the soft voices, the high and the low, the young and the old voices are like a choir that's singing to the accompaniment of the auctioneer's loud, monotonous drone.

But I've seen other rituals too. In the Midwest a teacher brought his art class to visit an old abandoned farm. Despite its weathered siding and its cobwebs, some students were captivated by the barn's classic lines, some by the effect of light and shadow through the barn windows and the cobwebs, and others by a rusted door hinge. So they painted the barn and had an art show. A thousand people came to see their exhibit. The barn had a purpose again.

I walked through another farm with a family. We stopped in dozens of places as they told me stories of their long life in that place.

I know a woman who returned to her homestead, when she was older, to reconstruct her childhood feelings and history. She walked through the property with her aged father, reviewed emotions and stories she'd almost forgotten, and grew closer to her father again. It was a time of renewal.

If my family were leaving a farm, I'd probably sculpture something symbolic, using metal scraps from old machinery. My friend would take pictures and create a photo story.

What can you imagine yourself doing at the end of a farm pilgrimage?

The drummers' pilgrimage

The pair played the drums well. They didn't know it, but they could play everything recorded in the Scriptures on those drums. So I gave them spur-of-the-moment instructions.

First drummer: Drum the mood of water, running water, a river. The river is the Jordan. *Second drummer:* Drum the mood of a person walking along that shoreline, into the water, up to the waist. The person is Jesus.

First drummer: Drum the water receiving the wind—wind and water in tension. The water is from God, and the wind is from God. The word of God is in the wind, and Jesus is inside both the water and the word. *Second drummer:* Drum Jesus as the wind and water, all in one motion, move around him, over him, overwhelm him, hold him, release him.

First drummer: Drum the emotion of the water, moving down the Jordan—a hundred feet wide, cool from the mountains, moving around the person of Jesus. *Second drummer:* Drum Jesus hearing a voice—from above, from within—saying, "You are my beloved."

First drummer: Drum the voice saying, "You are my beloved." *Second drummer:* Drum what Jesus thinks and feels as he hears that he is beloved.

The event was the drummers' pilgrimage. They interpreted a journey story and gave cadence to the stations in the pilgrimage.

Get into your pilgrimage

You are part of a pilgrimage. You can make it come alive.

Chant as you go. Call out words in pairs. Throw them back and forth like a ball: *vine* and *branches; bride* and *groom; inside, outside; sin* and *grace; good* and *evil; wind* and *water.* As you chant, feel the flow, the connection, the fellowship all around you. On tiptoe you go among battered and bruised ones. Dachau may be only a block off this route. Feel that you are one with hosts of saints and angels. Life flows from the vine through the branches. Your roots go deep and carry all you need to the very tips of your fingers.

Turn your face to the wind. It's more than moving air. Listen for silence. It's alive. In the mystery of the wind and the tidal waves, in the silent markings of DNA birthrights and signs inside chromosomes lurks the reminder: *I am the Lord your God, who rescues you from your slavery.* Turn your face to the wind and the silence and hear the word of pardon: *I forgive you because of who I am.*

Take off your shoes, for the place where you stand is a holy place. You came barefoot into life. There is nothing that can protect you forever from the earth. Step on the stones and the sand, on the broken glass and the cement, on the lawn and the meadow. This isn't a play. It's a pilgrimage.

Dig your toes into your pilgrimage. Get hold to run if you must. Then, in the sand where you walk, lean back on your heels and rest yourself while you stand upright. Dig in. Stand tall.

Splash your face and feet with water. Remember the water that's too deep for you to save yourself. A rainbow in the sky and a promise bigger than skyscrapers say "You'll not lose your way or your life."

Pick up a cross. Let its image surround you. Let it fill you up. Feel the cross stretch your skin until it cracks. Can you feel the cracking of the cross, too? There are times when the cracks in our lives are so big there seems to be nothing left but to cry and to curse. It is Jesus' cross that you carry, but he carries your curse. The cross is empty.

So toss up balloons as you break bread and drink wine. Sing "O Sacred Head Now Wounded," but whistle between the stanzas, for you know about Easter.

A mountain place

In a certain spirit-filled mountain village, a bus comes and goes each day. There is much hugging and waving and many tears of hello and good-bye. Each year pilgrims meet in this high mountain place. They travel far to get here. They bring many stories. Some they've never told before. And they leave with new stories to tell.

The joy in this pilgrim village springs from the rugged mountains, the hiking and climbing, the paint and clay, the stories, the prayer. But the mystique of this mountain place is created by the daily arrival of the bus that brings new visitors to the village and takes others away to the boat on the lake below.

We all are nomads. We all travel over lakes and mountains to meet somewhere for another holy station—another meeting place with God. Pilgrims on the move often meet those whom they least expect and most need.

Stations of the cross

Some pilgrims make a yearly pilgrimage by following the stations of the cross—places that mark specific events in the passion of Christ. Some of the fourteen traditional stations are Jesus taking up his cross, Jesus falling as he carries the cross, Jesus being nailed to the cross, Jesus dying on the cross, and Jesus being laid in the tomb.

When I was a boy, I knew such places. They were in the cemetery where I mowed the grass. The events in Christ's passion were recorded in the statues and in the verses and stories inscribed on the gravestones.

Another cemetery I visited had fourteen statues along a winding path. Each wooden statue depicted a part of Jesus' life that took place between Good Friday and Easter. When people visit the graves in this cemetery, they also walk the path of Jesus' suffering and resurrection. It reminds them of their own pilgrimage of victory over suffering and death.

In another town I saw families bring homemade banners down the aisle of their church during the offertory. The parade of banners told a story of the people's pilgrimage, for each banner represented a family's view of Holy Week. Together the banners depicted a pilgrimage of suffering and victory.

An older woman showed me a pillow that she had carefully embroidered. I could tell that she knew the events in the passion time of Jesus' life, for they were all stitched into the pillow.

In the stations of the cross we celebrate the triumph of Jesus. We meet God and ourselves in the mysteries of our faith. Any place, any event, any person can be a station—can point us to God and to an understanding of our own quest.

Journey with songs

Pilgrims create songs along the way. They have sunrise songs and midday and sunset songs. They have different tunes for different moods. They use simple words for big ideas, words with hidden meanings, and words that rhyme. Their songs are stories, to which they add new stanzas from time to time.

Pilgrims sing rhymed words like *revelation, incarnation, inspiration, confrontation, expectation, crucifixion, resurrection, celebration, congregation, dedication.*

Or they create lyrics from words like *trinity, energy, history, majesty, ecstasy, prophecy, constancy.*

They connect words like *night* and *light*, *bread* and *fed*, *kite* and *fight*, *wine* and *dine*, *loss* and *cross, grave* and *save*. They rhyme other words and wonder if they belong together— words like *good* and *wood, tree* and *free, sky* and *why, walk* and *talk, lamb* and *am, sword* and *lord, bring* and *sing, fear* and *hear, raise* and *praise*.

Pilgrims put their journey together, and they often do it with new songs.

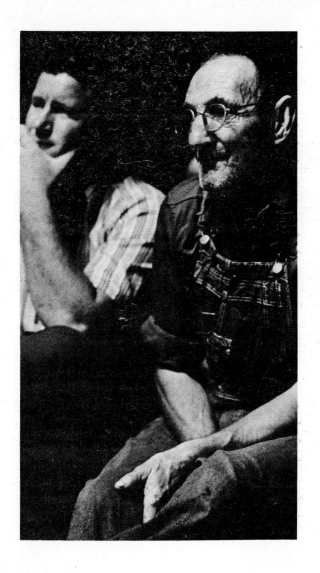

Chapter 3

Pilgrimage people

Pilgrimage in room 501

Jim lived in room 501. I saw him as often as possible. He'd been a carpenter for twenty-six years. The room was made of cement, and Jim missed the feel of wood, of the earth.

The first time we visited, Jim recalled the meadow that was once beneath this high building. As a young man he'd walked there. Each time we visited, he'd say, "Take me to the meadow." So we'd close our eyes and hold hands, and in our imaginations we'd drop down five stories onto a meadow. In our fantasy we'd stand on the land under and around the building. Each visit to the meadow was a station on our way.

One day we went to the meadow and prayed the Shepherd's Psalm. We saw two pictures: one of protection in the meadow and one of protection in a tent, where we stood before a full table while the enemy outside stood looking on. We told stories about times of danger and of protection.

Wherever I went, I told about the man in room 501. Young people around the country sent gifts with me for this carpenter. They whittled gifts and sent carved wood replicas of tools. They sent him a wooden lamb that knelt and bowed its head and danced, if you pressed it just right. One November day he opened many of these gifts. It felt like Christmas.

Once I took him a snowball I'd hidden inside my coat pocket. Then Jim talked about his many winters as a carpenter and told how he missed the cold and climbing onto the rooftops. His story was more like a winter journey than a brief visit. Down on the imaginary meadow we held the snowball until it melted.

Some college people heard about the carpenter. They sent him a twig from a campus oak tree. He held the twig as though it were a magic mirror. Pondering it, he said, "It is straight; it is strong; it will not break." He seemed to be speaking of himself. The twig helped him find the words he wanted to say.

A retired farmer sent him straw at Christmastime. Jim was thankful that out in the big winter world a farmer had thought of him in room 501. He used the straw as a bookmark.

Each time we visited, he said, "Go with me to the meadow." On the pilgrimage up in room 501, we traveled through a long shadowy valley and then through death.

A young man playing "Amazing Grace" on the bagpipes led the funeral procession. Months later a minister played "Beautiful Savior" on Jim's carpenter saw. Thousands sang along. Jim's journey still went on.

The pilgrimage of room 501 is not yet over.

Christian and Hopeful

In the book *Pilgrim's Progess,* Christian and his friend Hopeful see the gate to paradise. But between them and the gate is a very deep river. They can't find a bridge. To arrive at the gate, they must go through the deep water, knowing that the water will be as deep or as shallow as their belief in the king who lives beyond the gate.

When Christian goes down into the water, the waves come over his head. He fears he won't get to the promised land. Hopeful's feet touch the bottom of the river, so he encourages Christian with words of faith until Christian shouts, "I see him again."

Now Christian's faith makes his feet touch the ground too, and soon the water becomes shallow.

When Christian and Hopeful come out of the river on the other side, they walk toward paradise to see the tree of life, to eat its fruit that is always fresh, to talk to the king, and to never again know sorrow, sickness, pain, or death. They wear crowns of gold and white robes of glory and majesty. They hear God's voice and praise him with shouting and thanksgiving.

The water used in baptism symbolizes our descent into the deep waters. In our pilgrimage through this river, we lose our old self and are reborn. As we walk through the water, we discover who we are—we see ourselves. Some cry for fear, and only later do their feet find the ground. Some, like Hopeful, find the bottom quickly and know that everything is good.

Baptism is a journey of continual awareness. The pilgrimage teaches travelers who they are.

A baptism pilgrimage

How is baptism a pilgrimage? How can one brief act begin a long journey?

I remember a baptism pilgrimage in a Texas congregation. The people said, "There'll be a baptism while you're here. Do you mind?"

"Mind? Oh no. I can hardly wait. Who's the child?"

"Israel. His parents were born in Mexico."

I'd never been to Mexico. It was eleven miles to a border town. I went there to buy Israel a pair of sandals for his baptism. I saw the ones I wanted. As I paid the woman, she asked about his age. "Newborn," I said.

"These are for a ten year old," she commented.

But I liked them and told her about Israel's baptism.

"Don't worry," she said. "He'll grow."

Baptism is a pilgrimage of growth. Baptism is a line, a way—not just a dot. Little Israel will grow. He'll grow into those sandals. He'll be part of that line.

Israel slept during his baptism. He didn't see me give him the sandals or hear me tell the story of the lady in Mexico. But his father and mother were wide awake. For the first time they seemed to see baptism as a walk. They saw Israel moving toward ten years, and then on from there. Baptism is a way of life that we're on and in and about.

Two months later I visited the congregation again.

"Lisa will be baptized Sunday," they said. "She's Israel's cousin."

So I went shopping in Mexico again. I fell in love with yellow booties, small and fuzzy. As I paid for them, the woman asked, "How old is she?"

"Very little," I replied. "Three months."

"They're too small," she said.

I told her they were for Lisa's baptism.

"Don't worry," she counseled. "Tell her to hang them on the wall to remind her that she was baptized."

That's what I did. That's what it's all about. Baptism is going somewhere, being on the way. Baptism is living between remembering and growing into. It's being between the tiny booties and the bigger sandals. We're all on this pilgrimage with Lisa and Israel.

Terror and song

A nation and an army with chariots and the finest war horses were pursuing the pilgrims. Wheels sharp as swords churned swiftly through the fields and chopped up the earth. The pilgrims wished they had never headed for the land flowing with milk and honey.

"Don't be afraid," their leader said. "Stand your ground, and you will see what the Lord will do to save you today." This leader walked with a rod or a stick. It was a sign of the strength the pilgrims could receive from God, who had promised, "The Lord will fight for you, and all you have to do is keep still."

So Moses, their leader, stretched his hand over the sea, and God drove back the waters with a strong east wind. When the people had walked through the sea and were on the other side, the waters covered the pursuing horsemen and their chariots.

Then Moses' sister Miriam took up her tambourine and danced. Many of the pilgrims followed behind her, playing their tambourines and dancing. On the sandy shore of the Red Sea, saved from their terror, they sang out alleluias like Miriam's song.

I will sing to the Lord, for he has
   triumphed gloriously;
the horse and his rider he has thrown into
   the sea.

Exodus 15:1

A pilgrim town

A pilgrim town, I call it. It's like any town. Pilgrimages come and go within it, enter and leave its boundaries. But in this town the people think about what's happening, and later they share their ideas. So I came to their country town and joined the trek.

A boy of thirteen years took me to a lake. He showed me where his great-grandfather's farm had stood and told the story of a wheat binder buried under the water through the years. His great-grandfather had left it there when the lowland was a field. To leave the binder in the last field harvested was the custom. But the next spring's rains had filled the valley, and the lake has been there ever since. Someday the boy will dive beneath the water and raise the harvest binder. That is his dream.

Two young persons home from college took me to their family's dry-cleaning shop. Once it had been their father's. Now it was taking them three years to close and sell it. We ran across the alley and through the back door, the way they'd done when they were little. For two hours they spoke of the work and good times and feelings they'd had there. They told how it felt now to sell the machines for scrap metal. Being with them was like standing in a living scrapbook. Rewalking their history gave them nerve to go ahead.

A boy in this country town took me to an abandoned farm. He showed me a truck he'd inherited. When he was older, he'd fix it and get it running again. We looked at the old house that would soon be torn down. The boy had learned photography in 4-H. He took pictures so he'd remember the old farmstead. He showed me the ten rows of trees that make a windbreak for the house and told about each kind of tree. The boy kept his eye on the past and on the future, as though he understood them both.

The pilgrimage in this country town wouldn't stop. A girl told about a disease that almost took her life. It wasn't a simple story, and soon her father joined in the telling, speaking freely about death. Then her mother showed me a childhood painting she had done thirty years before. She still remembered the grade she'd received. It wasn't a high grade, yet she'd proudly hung the painting in her living room. The girl's story had turned the conversation into a journey.

A woman showed me the home where eighty older people live. Every Thursday she goes there to help them with their hair. She does it free, for a smile. She brings joy to that place. It's a place she knows well in this small pilgrimage town. I met two men in this home—two roommates. Their ages added up to one hundred and ninety-eight years. They wanted to talk about their past: where the church had first stood, how they had moved it. They pointed through the window to the valley they had come to at the turn of the century, and they pointed to the old, worn Bible lying on a nearby table. These men knew about journeys.

A person known as the town drunk spent each day packaging bird seed at the mill. This work was his pride and joy. He wanted to talk. There wasn't enough time on this town pilgrimage to hear all he wanted to tell or to visit all the places he liked most.

A young girl was trying to get used to the idea of her boyfriend leaving for military service. He would be going in two days. They hardly knew how to act, with so little time left. They had a lot to say and ask and promise. They were on their own pilgrimage that weekend.

A young man showed me ten acres of land that was his. He was preparing the ground for sowing millet. His mother had died, and he was having fainting spells that frightened the family. The man looked forward to going to the Mayo Clinic, but he was scared. The end of his journey was uncertain.

A woman who had recently emigrated from Europe was lonesome for her old home. She eagerly showed me pictures of her hometown. She cried a little, baked a cake, and showed me the porch her husband had built onto their house.

The minister in this small town played his

saxophone for me. The people had never heard him play. He'd been afraid to play ever since fourth grade, when his saxophone reed had squeaked. He remembered how the people had laughed and how terrible he had felt. That was twenty-eight years ago.

He played "Beautiful Savior," and the congregation sang along. This celebration completed my country-town pilgrimage.

A town is always on a pilgrimage. But some people don't know it. Go to a town. Ask what's happening. If the people say "Nothing," don't believe them. Look further. And listen.

Streetwise pilgrims

Some pilgrims are streetwise. They know how to survive in the city, how to be on their own, how to get along. They know about everyday living among the con artists. They are caught in the class struggle and have researchers studying them.

Streetwisdom is making it from day to day on the street. It's being able; it's coping and not being taken for a ride.

In their pilgrimage the streetwise have invented new ways to use old buildings. They've learned to make themselves at home for a while on hot cement, to explore vacant buildings, and to figure out what might happen next. They know when something is going on behind them, and they see how things fit together.

The streetwise get what they need. Surviving is a talent. Survival is their light that shines—on a rooftop or up a staircase or in an alley. These may be their hilltops.

The streetwise dream and wish. Blacktop is their sandlot. A recessed doorway has many uses. Hopscotch can be a trip. Rooftops become their penthouses.

The streetwise are practical. They use what's available. They know the journey itself is what's important.

My pilgrimage

I went on a memory pilgrimage and saw a lot of pictures.

I saw myself planting seeds and being frustrated because I didn't see how they could possibly grow.

I saw myself on a canoe trip, asking, "When are we going to get there?" Someone replied that "there" was just around the next bend. But then there was the next bend, and the next, and the next.

I saw myself in a boat. I saw other people sailing by, and I wanted to say, "Don't go by. Come into my boat. Come and sail with me awhile."

I saw myself climbing up a rocky slope, over huge boulders. I kept climbing to the next boulder, but it seemed just like the one I'd conquered before—only in a slightly different shape.

I saw counselors and elders—people who'd already been where I wanted to go, people who told me how they'd handled the situation.

I saw myself tempted and under peer pressure. I thought about doing something really crazy. With the temptation came testing and doubting. Then when I was more comfortable again, I doubted even more. But when I doubted, I looked closer at things. That kept my faith going. God was always there. He helped me cope.

I saw myself skiing. There were a lot of deer out in the woods. When I'd look down, I'd miss them, but when I looked up and watched closely, I saw twelve of them. I was in tune with the life in the woods.

My pilgrimage circles. It's not like a time line. Things keep repeating. Sometimes I'm speechless. I feel as though I've been there before.

On my pilgrimage I want to be in the middle of what's happening, not sitting at the end of a row in the bleachers. I want to submerge myself among people, to be a leader who's in the mix.

What is your pilgrimage like? How do you see your journey?

Chapter 4

Pilgrimage ways

Nature ways

Nature offers many opportunities for a pilgrimage. An eclipse is such a time. The smell of flowers is another. I like to smell the fresh apple blossoms in the spring. When I was little, I liked the smell of hollyhocks, too.

The first snowfall, the shortest night of the year, or a full moon—all these invite pilgrims to party. Nature supplies good pilgrimages.

But nature also brings times of danger and fear. Bad weather, fire, flood, and new seasons challenge my pilgrim courage. The worlds of nature and people are closely entwined.

Jewish days began and ended with sunset. So days began with rest. For most of us, this is a new way to approach a day.

Once I thought I'd forgotten what a sunrise looked like, so I got up early on twelve consecutive mornings and took pictures of the sun bursting into the new day. Then I discovered I'd forgotten to load the camera with film. But I saw the twelve sunrises.

I need to watch the clouds, to see their ever-changing shapes and moods. Sometimes I think I must see and feel the sunlight. These are pilgrim gifts. They are extravagant accessories, free for the pilgrim's taking. Is it possible that we are as rich as Jesus said? Is the kingdom of heaven really as near as birds in nests and lilies in the field?

All forms of life are on one grand pilgrimage. Heaven and earth do belong together. Nature and people can travel as friends.

The city way

I asked many young people what they saw when I talked about a pilgrimage through a city. They said they imagined pitched tents, people carrying an ark, singing, dancing, going through a playground, resting along the way. And they saw pilgrimage groups breaking bread—snacks of nuts and dried fruit—and a donkey leading a parade.

They paused. I asked them to think about other ordinary, simple sights—like the single donkey. Then they imagined how it would feel to carry a cross—to travel simply, with only a totebag to hold your belongings. They saw people serving each other—a car stopping and the driver jumping out to help push a stalled car; a city fire worker throwing candy to pilgrims in the streets.

There was another lull. I thought about the people who caught the candy. Then I asked, "What could they do to pass on the gift?" They answered, "Clean up the paper litter, help sandbag in flood times, paint the walls of abandoned neighborhood buildings."

I wondered how they pictured the end of the pilgrimage. They imagined the people joining with their fellow pilgrims in one last meal—holy communion.

Do you live in a city? What sights do you see along your way?

Spirit, come

Spirit, bring the mountains low
till yellow grains in meadows blow.
Spirit, raise the valleys high
till deep ravines reach to the sky.
Spirit, make the crooked straight
till pilgrims glimpse the golden gate.
Spirit, build the weary strong
till all their grieving turns to song.
Spirit, make the rebel still
till "No, I won't" becomes "I will."
Spirit, shine upon the night
till all our darkness turns to light.
Spirit, speak your holy word
till plowshares rise from melted sword.
Spirit, guide us day by day;
help us follow Christ, the Way.
Spirit, be our light and sage
on our endless pilgrimage.

And the lame walked

They all lay in a row in their hospital beds.
They couldn't walk, but they could still go on
a pilgrimage whenever they wished. One of
the nurses often led them. She'd take the
beat of a pulse and tap out its rhythm on the
bedstead. As others joined, the ward soon
felt the strong, beating sounds of pilgrimage.

They couldn't walk, but in their
imaginations they hurried up Mount Moriah
with Abraham and Isaac. They went up the
hill to the Temple with Hannah and Samuel.
They rushed through the Red Sea with the
nation of Israel and then kept walking,
walking, walking for forty years through the
desert. They ran away from home with
Jacob, and later they joined his son Joseph in
that long journey to the land of the
Pharaohs. They felt the time pass as the
prophets waited for the Messiah.

The tapping of the ward's huge rhythm
section sometimes led them to sing "We
Three Kings of Orient Are"; they marched
with the cadence of kings and of queens.
When they sang "We Are One in the Spirit,"
they felt that the whole ward was one.
Sometimes the rhythm led them to chant
psalms that helped them scale mountains and
walk valleys.

They couldn't walk—their bodies wouldn't
let them—but with this kind of leader they
could go anywhere, scale any mountain, ford

any river, and watch vistas on tiptoe. The
nurse knew how to get them into the
journey. She knew that the pilgrimage
cadence is deep inside the human spirit.

To wonder on the way

Where have the stars of winter been,
now that they shine clear again?
When we wave to say good-bye,
what begins and what will die?
Why do birthday parties seem
like distant, tiny, hazy dreams?
What do little persons know
when they stare and ponder so?
Where does all the journey end
when people rush around the bend?
Why do starlings stand so still
outside a winter windowsill?
What is hid so deep in me
that no one else will ever see?

A baptism journey

Baptism calls us to a journey that is a
continual pilgrimage. We're involved in the
journey from head to toe. The mark of the

water and the sign of the cross are on the body and head. We didn't put them there, and they won't disappear. We're enlisted in a long journey.

We go in and through deep places in this pilgrimage. We walk over and around and through high places. Sometimes our heads are in the heavens. Sometimes our feet touch the floor of deep waters.

God's spirit still moves over the creation. Out of weakness the spirit creates strength. Out of chaos the spirit forms new order. Out of death the spirit calls forth life.

We participate in this activity. We speak on this journey. It is our own pilgrimage. In places where we cry for help, we can also say hurrah. The journey is sometimes called the story of salvation.

A faith history walk

Three annual treks of the Israelites ended in Jerusalem. These worship experiences were scheduled to coincide with agricultural events. With lambing and barley harvest came Passover. With the wheat harvest came Pentecost. With the harvest of grapes, figs, and olives came the Feast of Booths. So each time the pilgrims traveled to Jerusalem, they took along an offering of produce.

And on each feast the Israelites recollected
what God had done for them. At Passover
they remembered their exodus from Egypt.
At Pentecost they recalled God's covenant
with them at Sinai, and how they had
become Yahweh's people. In the Feast of
Booths they remembered the wilderness
wandering.

Each year the people walked through
Israel's history so they'd know they were
part of that old journey of faith. And
through their own pilgrimage, they made
their history new.

Today, the history of faith keeps growing
as we add to it our own journeys of
recollection, experience, and worship.

Jerusalem songs

When the pilgrims of Israel came into
Jerusalem at the end of their pilgrimage to
the Holy City, they sang "psalms of
ascension." The lyrics painted pictures of
"gates lifting up their heads." These were
uphill songs.

Chant or read responsively some of the
uphill lyrics they sang. Or write your own
melodies for these old words. Match your
spirit to the uphill feelings of the pilgrims.

I lift up my eyes to the hills.
    From where does my help come?
My help comes from the Lord,
    who made heaven and earth.

Psalm 121:1-2

I was glad when they said to me,
    "Let us go to the house of the Lord!"
Our feet have been standing
    within your gates, O Jerusalem!

Psalm 122:1-2

To thee I lift up my eyes,
    O thou who art enthroned in the heavens!

Psalm 123:1

Those who trust in the Lord are like
  Mount Zion,
    which cannot be moved, but abides forever.

Psalm 125:1

A caravan journey

It was the boy's first trip to the big city—his first chance to come before God in a room so big that a hundred houses could fit under its roof.

Many people were making this journey. They played and ate and slept along the way. They were going to a feast. This boy knew his life had been saved long ago, in some miracle in Egypt. His parents had told him the story again and again, and he was grateful. He was young, but he seemed to know what it meant to be saved.

What a pilgrimage—to go to the big city, to travel with other families in a large caravan, to eat in new places along the way, to buy barley bread still warm from the oven, to bring along a pet lamb or a bird. To see the newborn lambs on the hillsides, kicking their hooves into the air; to see shepherds everywhere, watching their sheep. To meet learned people who'd surely tell stories both true and wise, to hear people discuss the future, to meet prophets, to chant and sing ballads. To see the sun set in valleys, making little towns stand like mysterious silhouettes on the hilltops, to walk near whitewashed tombstones, being careful not to touch them and become contaminated, to camp under the stars—and to wish.

The boy was curious. He was glad when he met teachers at the end of the journey. As the days passed, each conversation became more interesting, and he soon lost all sense of time.

After the feast the caravan prepared to head home. But the boy went to talk some more with the authors and editors and teachers who produced many of the writings for the city library and the schools. The learned people took him into their school.

Sometimes he walked with them under high ceilings, but mostly they all sat on big chairs and paged through stories on long manuscript pages called scrolls. The boy's understanding surprised these educated people, for he was only twelve.

They were in the Temple. In Jerusalem. It was the Feast of the Passover. For three days and three nights the excitement was so great that the boy didn't even miss his family. Thus did Jesus pilgrimage.

Chapter 5

Pilgrimage connections

The walking stick

We were three hundred youth on a weekend
pilgrimage—in a hotel. We took a fantasy
walk, telling stories along the way.

We had a walking stick, which we leaned
on when talking about some biblical or
current event. Leaning on the stick put us
pilgrims on location. It helped us all take part
in the story as it unfolded.

Near the end of the pilgrimage we
decorated the walking stick. Soon rainbow
colors twisted around its staff. Hanging on
this rainbow were many tiny, colorful cloth
symbols of the stories we had told: a
sparrow, a Detroit bus, a rock, a seed
sprouting. They reminded us of the good places
where we had stopped in our journey.

A pilgrimage can be an expensive journey
to France or to Mexico. Or a pilgrimage can
be stories so real and alive that all you need
are symbols tied to a walking stick to remind
you of them.

Homemade

Beside still waters
in sky, on highways
I play the flute and harp
with pilgrims
and sing to God a homemade song.

Beneath high steeples
and water towers
I rest my feet and soul
with Jesus
and tell to God my homemade thoughts.

Among the people
in bright orange sunsets
I take my bread and wine
with lovers
and praise my God in homemade love.

Come, Lord Jesus, be my host
and send to earth the Holy Ghost.

The church aisle

Pilgrim people see connections. In the
pilgrimage the same path connects the altar
and the corner drugstore. The church carpet
blends into the pavement outside.

The walk from the altar doesn't end at the
door. The church aisle is connected to the
classroom and the skating rink. Some
pilgrims can see the altar candles from the
grocery store. And if the pilgrim listens well,
the rhythm of the disco comes through at
the offertory.

The church aisle is an important aspect of
the journey. The pilgrimage is all one piece.

The church bell

There is a town where the church bell rings only once during the week. Nobody knows when it will ring. The time is a surprise to the people. On Sunday the members of the congregation come to church early so they can tell each other where they were when the bell rang. They talk about their week and about themselves. So these people feel close to each other, even though they spend most of their lives apart.

The members of this congregation cannot travel one by one along the route where each of them works, so they leave their work and gather together to tell their stories. When they're done listening to one another's stories, they feel as though they've all been on a pilgrimage together.

The church bell reminds them that they do not journey alone.

Pilgrim rocks

On one long journey the pilgrims carried tiny rocks in their hands. As they touched and handled the rocks, they came to know them by heart. The rocks kept them in touch with life. Holding the rocks kept them close to mountains and brooks, to pebbles under their feet, and to stars overhead. The little stones reminded them of places they'd been to and

loved in the past. So they felt more at ease
with these rocks clasped tightly in their
hands.

The pilgrims made up stories about their
rocks and told them to each other. They
began to feel more like brothers and sisters.

Some of the people exchanged rocks with
each other. They felt the spirit of giving and
receiving in their pilgrimage. It was a
celebration. They felt like singing Christmas
songs.

Once they held the rocks and sang a little
rock song.

> Little rock, little rock,
>   where have you been?
> When the earth was hot and new,
>   where were you, rock,
>   where were you?
> Little rock, little rock,
>   where have you been?

Another time they piled their rocks
together and had a memorial service. Each
rock honored someone special. Some pilgrims
told stories. After the service each person
took back a rock from the pile and started
walking again, remembering the stories and
the feeling of honoring others.

Later, some pilgrims skipped their rocks
over lakes and the edges of oceans, and they
made wishes. Some dropped their rocks into
deep caves and old cisterns, and hoped.

The people of Israel gathered twelve
stones, one for each tribe, and placed them

in the middle of the Jordan River as a remembrance of how God had helped them move the ark of the covenant into the Promised Land. Their leader, Joshua, explained the importance of their act.

> In the future, when your children
> ask you what these stones mean,
> you will tell them about the time
> when Israel crossed the Jordan on
> dry ground. Tell them that the
> Lord your God dried up the Red Sea
> for us. Because of this everyone on
> earth will know how great the Lord's
> power is, and you will honor the
> Lord your God forever.
>
> Joshua 4:21-24

A pilgrim's cafe

A small cafe is one of the places along the pilgrimage. Many persons meet there every day to reflect, to tell, to listen, to stare, to forget, to care.

How do you picture a cafe? Do you see the people there as pilgrims?

Try thinking about a cafe as an oasis along a journey. Next time you stop at such a cafe, notice how the people treat one another. Do you get a feeling of hospitality? Take a second look at the pilgrims you know. Do you see them in a new light?

Study those who are strangers. Guess something about the life of each one. How does the behavior and conversation of the "regulars" affect the strangers? Does it warm their spirits? Does it make them feel even more left out? Be alert for the chance to become acquainted with one of them in a caring way.

Once a waitress saw me feverishly writing as I ate breakfast. Her brother managed the cafe, and she was proud of his work. She was less sure about herself. She talked about her talent and need to write. She said our meeting—seeing me work and telling me her story—made it a good day in her erratic life. Since then many restaurants across the country have become my favorite writing places.

Have you ever been grateful for a pilgrim's cafe?

Other candles

Some friends could not describe their pilgrimage. When they took pictures of their activities, they found that their pilgrimage was all around them. They just hadn't noticed. They were inside their journey and didn't know it.

The cameras focused on the pilgrims and the events in their pilgrimage. The pilgrims worried that there wouldn't be enough people to take pictures of. But there wasn't enough film. There was so much to shoot; the wide-angle lenses were too narrow.

When the people saw the pictures, their eyes had a banquet. They had feared they would go hungry, but instead they feasted. What the cameras hadn't filmed reminded the pilgrims of the crumbs at the feeding of the five thousand. So much was left over. More than they had started with.

The cameras were acolytes. They lit altar candles. Their bulbs flashed in the presence of God. God's people were close by.

I give thee what I have

Once there was a town whose people thought they could not give. They felt they had too little to share with those who passed through their town. They didn't know how to give what they had.

Then someone came to them who saw their need and gift wrapped their bread. Soon the people began to gift wrap their drink. Then they gift wrapped other common things: shoes and socks, eggs and toast, carrots and broccoli. They even put ribbons on their water faucets and trees and bicycles.

They took a fresh look at these things and saw them all as gifts. They learned to give, for they learned to see what they had.

Now these people look forward to giving to those who journey through their town.

Gifts

We receive presents when we go on a journey. The gifts come in many forms: bread, fish, rain, visitors, children, spouses, peace, memories, daily events, stories, special times. Some gifts are expected; some come by surprise. Some are for us to eat and drink or use along the way. Others are less tangible. There are sights never to be seen again. No way can be traveled exactly the same twice. There are new and true stories to hear. They become our gospel—our good news—just as stories about these gifts of God are at the heart of the Gospel.

As we travel into the unknown to make it known and look at something old until it becomes new, the presents keep coming. A sunrise may surprise us as if we'd never seen one before. A distant relative may become a friend. A stranger may become a sister or brother. A water fountain may put us in touch with stories about water.

The gifts are plentiful. But we can't hold all that is given to us. So we'll give away what we receive. We'll tell what was told to us. We'll show others what we saw.

Our pilgrim totes ought to be empty each morning. To receive is one part of pilgrimage.

The yes cross

The pilgrimage lasted for several hours. As hundreds of people moved through streets marked off for the journey, one sign was always among them: a huge cross. The presence of the cross was more than magic to them. Something comforting was happening. They felt affirmed.

They passed the cross overhead, from one to another as they walked, for they all wanted to touch it. They danced with it, and circling in groups around it, they made sounds of sorrow, wailed, and spoke of sad times and places. The cross seemed to give them energy, for they said words and sang songs about power and strength. They used it as an oar in a stormy sea while they told stories and sang songs about water, floods, and salvation. Some used it as a walking stick and told faith stories along the way. Others used it like a flag and waved it victoriously. Some carved markings into this cross. Others held it and sang prison songs or recalled Bible stories about being set free.

The cross had meaning for each of the pilgrims. Its presence told them that they were special and showed others that they were part of the pilgrimage of Jesus.

Finally the pilgrimage ended. The pilgrims put the cross down and rested. Then they raised it up again, decorated it like a Christmas tree, and sang about joy and birth, about peace and rebirth.

They named the cross Yes.

The sign of the cross

A girl saw the minister make the sign of the cross on the people. So she made the sign on her playmates and then on her toys.

She made the sign of the cross on her mother and father and on the people who rode on buses. She made the sign over her bed and on her favorite storybooks.

Sometimes she made the sign of the cross over her food, and the food tasted better to her.

When she was much older, she made the same sign over the body of her dying friend, who smiled and said, "We Christians do have this sign to see by." The sign of the cross reminded the woman and her dying friend of important things. The sign was what they needed to look ahead and not be afraid. It gave perspective to the pilgrimage.

Now the woman is a mother. And she makes the sign on her children. They are part of her lifelong pilgrimage.

Pilgrim's cloth

Pilgrims dress simply. They travel light.

Some take a pilgrimage cloth along. They use it for many things. With it they wipe faces and feet. They wave it for joy, tie it into an apron, spread it on a table, fold it for a pillow or spread it out for a blanket.

Whenever and however the pilgrim uses the cloth, it becomes something holy. It can become an altar cloth or a prayer rug.

Some pilgrims tie the corners of the cloth together to carry their simple belongings: their apples and little rocks and messages and feathers and souvenirs and bread. They tie these handmade tote bags to their hips or shoulders.

Pilgrims dress simply. But they soon learn that what they wear becomes very special.

If pilgrims can do all this with a cloth, think how many ways there must be to use a simple walking stick, a cross, a candle.

Little Rock

Soft and slow

Lois Brokering

Lit-tle rock, lit-tle rock, where have you been?

Lit-tle rock, lit-tle rock tell me what you've seen!

When the earth was hot and new,

where were you, rock, where were you?

Lit-tle rock, lit-tle rock, where have you been?

Order from Herb Associates, 11641 Palmer Rd., Minneapolis, MN 55437

Chapter 6

Pilgrimage insights and prayers

He who has eyes to see, let him see

For years Carl had looked at a certain tiny
piece of moss and imagined a rock, a tree, a
forest, a mountainside, a universe. That's the
way he thought. But he didn't mention it to
anyone, for he was sure it was a strange and
improper way to think. He was sixty-seven.

One day at the dinner table he talked
about the moss particle and described his way
of seeing things. All approved. They thought
that way too. They all looked at tiny things
and saw much more. In a little they saw a
lot. But they'd never told one another before.

Carl said that was the way he saw the
bread in Holy Communion. When the bread
was broken, and Carl saw the pieces being
shared, he also saw the congregation, the
hungry and the thirsty and those feasting,
and all meals and harvest fields and work and
factories, and the whole Church—the body of
Christ. One after another, the pictures
appeared in his imagination.

His mind would go on a visionary journey.
Looking at a tiny piece of bread, Carl could
be with all life and all people. He could move
from his small spot at the communion table
to the entire cosmic system. He understood
the images Jesus used. He could see the
mustard seed as a tree or watch a bird in
flight and let his imagination soar all the way

to the kingdom of heaven. Carl had the gift of being able to travel in his imagination.

A pilgrimage needs imagination.

A quest for knowledge

Where do fragile bluebirds go
when the forecast calls for snow?
Why do birds break autumn song
with a flight so high and long?

Why do daffodils bow down,
wilt so soon and turn so brown?
How does even winter earth
bring the daffodil rebirth?

Why do stories very old
seem like new though oft retold?
Why does information said
seem more real than if just read?

Why does every gracious prize
gently bring its own surprise?
What do different people see
when they look again at me?

Pilgrimage is a quest for knowledge. Asking questions along the way helps the pilgrim to see more clearly and more deeply.

Listening

At a huge festival a blind person asked her friend to explain what was happening on the stage. The friend described the water and songs and lambs and rainbows; the blind person said, "I see. Tell me more."

So the friend told about the potter and the weaver and the baptismal font and the prisoners. The blind person listened and saw it all. Then the friend told the blind person, "Even though you are blind, you've shown me the festival."

Listening and seeing go together. Listening is a journey of the senses. Listening makes us more aware.

As you listen to people talk, do you treat what they say as something new? Do you notice their tone of voice? As they speak, do you watch their faces and gestures, and those of the listeners?

I have been with people who say that nothing is happening around them. They're bored. So I ask them to join me and pretend that there is a play going on around us. I ask them to listen to one another describe the play. Now tiny things take on new importance for these people.

Have you ever watched a scene or an event come together? Have you ever listened to someone describe it? Have you ever listened to yourself describe it for another person?

Have you observed how persons arrive, how they are received or rejected? Have you noticed the hello words, and then the good-bye words?

Listening is essential for a meaningful pilgrimage. It's necessary for survival. And it gives us further reasons for celebrating.

A voice points a way

Those who listen as they go,
    hear a call they know is so.
Deep inside, as old as they,
    lies a voice that points a way.
Ask about the destiny
    of your pilgrim's history.
"What is it I want to be?
    What is it I wish to see?"
Choose the life you will achieve,
    what it is you will receive.
Walking in your unshod feet,
    sense the One you hope to meet.

Life's many levels

Life is deep and high. It's simple and complex. There's always activity on many levels at the same time. We walk the hot pavement of city streets while underground rivers flow beneath us, while insects and earthworm colonies cut their own highways through tunnels we'll never see. And all the while seed flies through the air, and the pollen mixes with particles of dust and with tiny droplets of moisture.

Just look; here comes a cloud. Feel the rain. There it goes to the other side of the road, and to the other side of town. I feel I'm inside a living world. It moves over me and through me. Rain is part of my heritage and my future. It's important in so many of the stories I know about God.

Follow the pilgrimage of nature. Look, there goes the smog. Here comes the sun and its warmth. There go the migrating geese. Look, there go the leaves, and there go the seasons. Look, there go your friends and your family. Times spent out-of-doors— hiking and walking and canoeing—run through my mind. The weather churns up emotions and energy in me. I want to join in the life of God's nature.

Life has diverse levels. Together they are one system. They are one piece, one body, one power, one kingdom. Together they radiate one glory.

Everything is on a journey. Together the layers of life create one story. For me there can be no future life apart from this life. All these levels—above and beneath and within

me—are the spaces where God's spirit moves.
The one Creator pervades and gives life to
the whole pilgrimage.

Gifts

Lord of queens and mighty kings,
endless oceans, tiny springs,
wash my face and tired feet,
gently cool the noonday heat;
cleanse my forehead and my hands;
calm all anxious pilgrim bands.
All the good that comes to me
comes as gifts, dear Lord, from thee.

A foretaste

A girl pressed her face against the smoked
glass window and waved furiously to her
father. To keep from crying she shouted
loudly, "Good-bye, good-bye, Daddy, Daddy,
Daddy."

Her mother sat quietly nearby. As the door
of the airplane closed, all three years of the
girl's life rolled over her like a fierce tidal
wave. Fear, love, and trust climaxed together
at once.

Her shouted good-byes dwindled to a whimper. But when the traumatic good-bye experience had faded into silence, she was ready for the next big wave, for the time when she'd cry out, "Hello, hello, Daddy, Daddy, Daddy."

In these good-byes and hellos, the young girl rehearses the many farewells and welcomes of her future. They are a foretaste of death and resurrection.

A child

There once was a child on the run
who turned to the west and the sun,
who rose on tiptoe
to watch the sun go—
to receive creation as fun.

A pilgrimage prayer

Lord, the pilgrimage is long.
Send my soul a walking song;
then I'll know that I belong
with your marching pilgrim throng.

Lord, the road to you is slow,
turning, twisting high and low.
I am lost unless you show
pilgrim feet the way to go.

Lord, my pilgrimage is done.
Thank you for the love and fun
and the joy of setting sun.
Thanks to you, my race is run.

Chapter 7

Pilgrimage endings

The end of a pilgrimage

"How do you think a pilgrimage might end?"
The answers were spontaneous.

"When you reach a goal, you should reflect and be happy."

"With lots of singing."

"I'd just feel that it was done and over with."

"With exaltation."

"It's a time for prayer."

"I like to have things wild at the end."

"I think of the song 'Let us break bread together.'"

"Arriving is a time for celebration—like Easter."

No load too heavy

They carried the coffin on their friend's pilgrimage. He was young, eighteen, as they were young. They carried him through this station on his journey. It took them two hours on a Friday.

The coffin was too heavy for them. They were strong. Some were weight lifters, and some were runners. But their dead friend was too heavy.

So they moved closer together, five inches each. Now there was space for one more friend. They simply marked that place with the sign of the cross. When they lifted the coffin again, they were able to carry their friend.

Jesus walked alongside the coffin in this pilgrimage. He lightened the burden of the young man's friends, just as he comforted the grieving mother in Nain.

Jesus is along on each pilgrimage. His presence releases our energy during the pilgrimage. There is no heavy burden that he will not help us carry.

Questions

Lord,
Why am I upon this way?
What do people think and say?
Will the journey end one day?

Why the cross and why my dread?
Must I soon lie with the dead?
Will it be on Easter bed?

Will I find a great surprise?
Will the journey make me wise?
Will I win the final prize?

Tell me what the prize will be.
Is it very hard to see?
Is it hid in mystery?

Will I reach the pilgrim goal?
What will heal my wounded soul?
What will make my spirit whole?

God, Creator, Lord, and King,
Hear this pilgrim's questioning;
Teach me, that my soul may sing.

Resting stations

In the Middle Ages certain resting stations
were called hospices. Pilgrims found healing
and nourishment at these stopping-off places.
They were their first-aid stations, their
restaurants, their motels, their telephone
booths, their mailboxes, their news reports.
   Today a hospice is still a place where
people on a journey can receive rest and
special care. It's a home for those away from
home. It's personal and intimate care, which
makes the person feel whole.
   Pilgrims need hospices along their way—
places to rest and nap, to find healing and
restoration. They need to stop in meaningful
places.
   Any town can be that place. A
congregation can be a hospice. Or a home
can.
   Hospice and hospitality are old notions
among travelers. Sarah and Abraham made

their tent a hospice. Their visitors were from
the Lord. The visit broke their barren life.
Isaac was born.

Praise the Lord

Praise the Lord with a waving hand,
   with a threefold yes,
   with snapping of fingers,
   with a sudden whistle,
   with stamping of feet.
Praise the Lord with a winking eye,
   with a loving kiss,
   with a harmonious hum,
   with clapping of hands.
Praise the Lord with a hearty laugh,
   with a handshake,
   with a deep breath,
   with a sigh.
Praise the Lord with a sure Amen.

Living symbols

There is a family who never cuts a tree for
Christmas. Instead they use eggs and ivy and
other living forms. They use these both for

Christmas and for Holy Week/Easter; they think deeply about what they do.

Once they put an egg beside a candle on a table. It was a sign of birth and rebirth at the same time. The tableau reminded them of Jesus' birthplace, so they sang "O Little Town of Bethlehem." When they sang "Were you there when they laid him in the tomb," it also seemed to fit. Later, they carefully warmed an egg, until it hatched. It was Easter.

One year during Advent they folded a towel around an ear of corn and put it beside a candle. They talked excitedly about the past summer and the good harvest—how it had been a bumper crop of corn. Later, each person received some kernels of corn as a gift. They were grateful and sang "I am so glad each Christmas eve, the night of Jesus' birth." Much later, they planted the kernels in a warm, lighted place indoors. When the corn sprouted and its new stalks poked their way through the soil into the light, they sang "Jesus Christ Is Risen Today. Alleluia!"

Another time they placed a large ivy plant beside a candle. They enjoyed its flowing vines, its green leaves, its life. One person told about how much it had grown since she received it. While they hummed "Angels, from the realms of glory, wing your flight o'er all the earth," she cut a slip for each of them. They felt in touch with the mystery of life, and they felt close to one another.

One Christmas they laid a new baby carefully beside a candle and were very quiet, for the baby slept. It was the softest they had ever sung "Silent Night, Holy Night." As they sang "Ah, Holy Jesus" on Good Friday, the baby slept again. Some of them understood the mood of pianissimo for the first time.

Another year the shoe of a young person who had left them became the candle's mate.

Each year this family adds a station to their Christmas-Easter pilgrimage, and they recall the stations they've passed through. Next year they'll set new wine beside a candle, for one in the family is learning to make wine. But when they meet, there will also be an egg, an ear of corn, an ivy plant, a child become a toddler, and a young person's shoe.

The candle is always there. It reminds them of the constant presence of Christ along their journey.

The everlasting hello and good-bye

Hello, bird.
Hello, sky.
Hello, tree.
Hello, wind.
Hello, bug.
Hello, sidewalk.

Hello, smashed worm.
Hello, door.
Good-bye, bird.
Good-bye, sky.
Good-bye, tree.
Good-bye, wind.
Good-bye, bug.
Good-bye, sidewalk.
Good-bye, smashed worm.
Good-bye, door.
Hello, mother.
Hello, father.

Pilgrimage is such a way of walking.

A child led the way

Each year the man joined some Easter
pilgrimage. This time he came to worship in
a home.

A girl greeted him as he entered the tiny
house where he would celebrate Easter. She
asked him to draw the name of a partner for
their Easter walk. "You get one, too," she
said. "We planned it that way."

He drew the name of Eric, age two.
Together they set out on their Easter
pilgrimage in the back yard. Eric smiled in a
way that made the man both wonder and
worry. So he grabbed for the boy's hand; but
Eric was gone.

Somewhere out in the tall grass Eric was shouting, "See!" He had found a rock, a little stone. How did a boy of two years know about a stone and Easter? The man was amazed. Eric was two, and he was busy finding something for the man to see. He gave the stone to the man as a gift.

Then the boy was off and looking again, repeatedly shouting, "See!"

And so the boy and the man looked down into the face of a flower, a dandelion. Eric plucked it and gave it to the man. Six minutes of pilgrimage, and they'd already visited stations of the rock and the flower.

Eric's recurrent "See!" rang through the Easter air. And then he was off again, running through the grass. His hands flew up as he fell, and now *he* was the gift to the man, who raised him to his shoulders. They were together—another station in their Easter pilgrimage.

They ran to the others in the house, with Eric still shouting, "See!" Now the family was all together—still another station in the pilgrimage. The man looked around in wonder and said, "See, Lord!"

Gifts of a rock and a flower, of a boy and a family—all these were there. On a pilgrimage everything counts. Each tiny thing is sacred. This pilgrimage was working. A child had made the journey holy.

I have triumphed gloriously

Yes, I have triumphed gloriously,
with the life of Christ in me
I have won victoriously;
death is drowned beneath the sea.
Jesus Christ is risen. Christ is risen today.

Yes, I have triumphed gloriously,
for resurrection life of thee
broke the grave majestically;
death is drowned beneath the sea.
Jesus Christ is risen. Christ is risen today.

Yes, I have triumphed gloriously
with Easter bread in front of me;
by this holy mystery
death is drowned beneath the sea.
Jesus Christ is risen. Christ is risen today.

(Sing to the tune "In Dulci Jubilo.")